CULTURE OF DANCE

MR VIVEK KUMAR PANDEY SHAMBHUNATH

Contents

CHAPTER ONE

.

"Dancer" and *"Dancing"* redirect here. For other uses, see *Dancer (disambiguation)*and *Dancing (disambiguation)*.

Performing arts

- Acrobatics
  - Ballet
- Circus skills
  - Clown
  - Dance

- General Gymnastics
  - Magic

  - Mime
  - Music
  - Opera

- Professional wrestling

  - Puppetry

  - Speech
  - Theatre
- Ventriloquism

- v
- t
- e

Two modern dancers

Members of a dance routine.

Dance is a performing artform consisting of purposefully selected sequences of human movement. This movement has aesthetic and symbolic value, and is acknowledged as dance by performers and observers within a particular culture.[nb 1] Dance can be categorized and described by its choreography, by its repertoire of movements, or by its historical period or place of origin.[4]

An important distinction is to be drawn between the contexts of theatrical and participatory dance,[5] although these two categories are not always completely separate; both may have special functions, whether social, ceremonial, competitive, erotic, martial, or sacred/liturgical. Other forms of human movement are sometimes said to have a dance-like quality, including martial arts, gymnastics, cheerleading, figure skating, synchronised swimming, marching bands, and many other forms of athletics.

Contents

Performance and participation

Members of an American jazz dance company perform a formal group routine in a concert dance setting

Theatrical dance, also called performance or concert dance, is intended primarily as a spectacle, usually a performanceupon a stageby virtuosodancers. It often tells a story, perhaps using mime, costumeand scenery, or else it may simply interpret the musical accompaniment, which is often specially composed. Examples are western balletand modern dance, Classical Indian danceand Chinese and Japanese song and dance dramas. Most classical forms are centred upon dance alone, but performance dance may also appear in operaand other forms of musical theatre.

Participatory dance, on the other hand, whether it be a folk dance, a social dance, a group dancesuch as a line, circle, chainor square dance, or a partner dancesuch as is common in western Western ballroom dancing, is undertaken primarily for a common purpose, such as social interactionor exercise, of participants rather than onlookers. Such dance seldom has any narrative. A group dance and a corps de ballet, a social partner dance and a pas de deux, differ profoundly. Even a solo dancemay be undertaken solely for the satisfaction of the dancer. Participatory dancers often all employ the same movements and steps but, for example, in the rave cultureof electronic dance music, vast crowds may engage in free dance, uncoordinated with those around them. On the other hand, some cultures lay down strict rules as to the particular dances in which, for example, men, women and children may or must participate.

Origins

Main article: History of Dance

Mesolithic dancers at Bhimbetka

Archeologicalevidence for early dance includes 9,000-year-old paintings in Indiaat the Rock Shelters of Bhimbetka, and Egyptiantomb paintings depicting dancing figures, dated c. 3300 BC. It has been proposed that before the invention of written languages, dance was an important part of the oral and performance methods of passing stories down from one generation to the next.[6]The use of dance in ecstatictrance statesand healing rituals (as observed today in many contemporary "primitive" cultures, from the Brazilian rainforestto the Kalahari Desert) is thought to have been another early factor in the social development of dance.[7]

References to dance can be found in very early recorded history; Greek dance(horos) is referred to by Plato, Aristotle, Plutarchand Lucian.[8]The Bibleand Talmudrefer to many events related to dance, and contain over 30 different dance terms.[9]In Chinesepottery as early as the Neolithicperiod, groups of people are depicted dancing in a line holding hands,[10]and the earliest Chinese word for "dance" is found written in the oracle bones.[11]Dance is further described in the Lüshi Chunqiu.[12][13]Primitive dance in ancient China was associated with sorcery and shamanic rituals.[14]

Greek bronze statuette of a veiled and masked dancer, 3rd–2nd century BC, Alexandria, Egypt.

During the first millennium BCEin India, many texts were composed which attempted to codify aspects of daily life. Bharata Muni's Natyashastra (literally "the text of dramaturgy") is one of the earlier texts. It mainly deals with drama, in which dance plays an important part in Indian culture. It categorizes dance into four types – secular, ritual, abstract, and, interpretive – and into four regional varieties. The text elaborates various hand-gestures (mudras) and classifies movements of the various limbs, steps and so on. A strong continuous tradition of dance has since continued in India, through to modern times, where it continues to play a role in culture, ritual, and, notably, the Bollywoodentertainment industry. Many other contemporary danceforms can likewise be traced back to historical, traditional, ceremonial, and ethnicdance.

Dance and music

Main article: Dance music

Dancing girls in pop-concert, Sofia, Bulgaria.

Dance is generally, though not exclusively, performed with the accompaniment of music and may or may not be performed in timeto such music. Some dance (such as tap dance) may provide its own audible accompaniment in place of (or in addition to) music. Many early forms of music and dance were created for each other and are frequently performed together. Notable examples of traditional dance/music couplings include the jig, waltz, tango, disco, and salsa. Some musical genreshave a parallel dance form such as baroque musicand baroque dance; other varieties of dance and music may share nomenclature but developed separately, such as classical musicand classical ballet.

Dance and rhythm

Rhythmand dance are deeply linked in history and practice. The American dancer Ted Shawnwrote; "The conception of rhythm which underlies all studies of the dance is something about which we could talk forever, and still not finish."[15]A musical rhythm requires two main elements; first, a regularly-repeating pulse(also called the "beat" or "tactus") that establishes the tempoand, second, a pattern of accentsand reststhat establishes the character of the metre or basic rhythmic pattern. The basic pulse is roughly equal in duration to a simple step or gesture.

A basic tango rhythm

Dances generally have a characteristic tempo and rhythmic pattern. The tango, for example, is usually danced in ^{2}

$_4$time at approximately 66 beats per minute. The basic slow step, called a "slow", lasts for one beat, so that a full "right–left" step is equal to one ^{2}

$_4$measure. The basic forward and backward walk of the dance is so counted – "slow-slow" – while many additional figures are counted "slow – quick-quick.[16]

Just as musical rhythms are defined by a pattern of strong and weak beats, so repetitive body movements often depends on alternating "strong" and "weak" muscular movements.[17]Given this alternation of left-right, of forward-backward and rise-fall, along with the bilateral symmetryof the human body, it is natural that many dances and much music are in duple and quadruple meter. However, since some such movements require more time in one phase than the other – such as the longer time required to lift a hammer than to strike – some dance rhythms fall equally naturally into triple metre.[18]Occasionally, as in the folk dances of the Balkans, dance traditions depend heavily on more complex rhythms. Further, complex dances composed of a fixed sequence of steps always require phrases and melodies of a certain fixed length to accompany that sequence.

Lululaund – The Dancing Girl (painting and silk cloth. A.L. Baldry 1901, before p. 107), The inscription reads; "Dancing is a form of rhythm/

Rhythm is a form of music/ Music is a form of thought/ And thought is a form of divinity."

The very act of dancing, the steps themselves, generate an "initial skeleton of rhythmic beats" that must have preceded any separate musical accompaniment, while dance itself, as much as music, requires time-keeping[19]just as utilitarian repetitive movements such as walking, hauling and digging take on, as they become refined, something of the quality of dance.[17]

Musical accompaniment therefore arose in the earliest dance, so that ancient Egyptians attributed the origin of the dance to the divine Athotus, who was said to have observed that music accompanying religious rituals caused participants to move rhythmically and to have brought these movements into proportional measure. The same idea, that dance arises from musical rhythm, is still found in renaissanceEurope in the works of the dancing master Guglielmo Ebreo da Pesarowho speaks of dance as a physical movement that arises from and expresses inward, spiritual motion agreeing with the "measures and perfect concords of harmony" that fall upon the human ear,[17]while, earlier, Mechthild of Magdeburg, seizing upon dance as a symbol of the holy life foreshadowed in Jesus' saying "I have piped and ye have not danced",[20]writes;

I can not dance unless thou leadest. If thou wouldst have me spring aloft, sing thou and I will spring, into love and from love to knowledge and from knowledge to ecstasy above all human sense[21]

Thoinot Arbeau's celebrated 16th century dance-treatise *Orchésographie*, indeed, begins with definitions of over eighty distinct drum-rhythms.[22]

Helen Moller

As has been shown above, dance has been represented through the ages as having emerged as a response to music yet, as Lincoln Kirsteinimplied, it is at least as likely that primitive music arose from dance. Shawn concurs, stating that dance "was the first art of the human race, and the matrix out of which all other arts grew" and that even the "metrein our poetry today is a result of the accents necessitated by body movement, as the dancing and reciting were performed simultaneously"[15]– an assertion somewhat supported by the common use of the term "foot" to describe the fundamental rhythmic units of poetry.

Scholes, not a dancer but a musician, offers support for this view, stating that the steady measures of music, of two, three or four beats to the bar, its equal and balanced phrases, regular cadences, contrasts and repetitions, may all be attributed to the "incalculable" influence of dance upon music.[23]

Émile Jaques-Dalcroze, primarily a musician and teacher, relates how a study of the physical movements of pianists led him "to the discovery that musical sensations of a rhythmic nature call for the muscular and nervous response of the whole organism", to develop "a special training designed to regulate nervous reactions and effect a co-ordination of muscles and nerves" and ultimately to seek the connections between "the art of music and the art of dance", which he formulated into his system of eurhythmics.[24]He concluded that "musical rhythm is only the transposition into sound of movements and dynamisms spontaneously and involuntarily expressing emotion".[25]

Hence, though doubtless, as Shawn asserts, "it is quite possible to develop the dance without music and... music is perfectly capable of standing on its own feet without any assistance from the dance", nevertheless the "two arts will always be related and the relationship can be profitable both to the dance and to music",[26]the precedence of one art over the other being a moot point. The common ballad measuresof hymns and folk-songs takes their name from dance, as does the carol, originally a circle dance. Many purely musical pieces have been named "waltz" or "minuet", for example, while many concert danceshave been produced that are based upon abstract musical pieces, such as *2 and 3 Part Inventions, Adams Violin Concerto*and *Andantino*. Similarly, poems are often structured and named after dances or musical works, while dance and music have both drawn their conception of "measure" or "metre" from poetry.

Shawn quotes with approval the statement of Dalcroze that, while the art of musical rhythm consists in differentiating and combining time durations, pauses and accents "according to physiological law", that of "plastic rhythm" (i.e. dance) "is to designate movement in space, to interpret long time-values by slow movements and short ones by quick movements, regulate pauses by their divers successions and express sound accentuations in their multiple nuances by additions of bodily weight, by means of muscular innervations".

Shawn nevertheless points out that the system of musical time is a "man-made, artificial thing.... a manufactured tool, whereas rhythm is something that has always existed and depends on man not at all", being "the continuous flowing time which our human minds cut up into convenient units", suggesting that music might be revivified by a return to the values and the time-perception of dancing.[27]

The early-20th-century American dancer Helen Moller stated simply that "it is rhythm and form more than harmony and color which, from the beginning, has bound music, poetry and dancing together in a union that is indissoluble."[28]

Approaches to dance

Concert dance

Concert dance, like opera, generally depends for its large-scale form upon a narrativedramatic structure. The movements and gestures of the choreographyare primarily intended to mimethe personality and aims of the characters and their part in the plot.[29]Such theatrical requirements tend towards longer, freer movements than those usual in non-narrative dance styles. On the other hand, the *ballet blanc*, developed in the 19th century, allows interludes of rhythmic dance that developed into entirely "plotless" ballets in the 20th century[30]and that allowed fast, rhythmic dance-steps such as those of the *petit allegro*. A well-known example is *The Cygnets' Dance*in act two of *Swan Lake*.

The balletdeveloped out of courtly dramatic productions of 16th- and 17th-century France and Italy and for some time dancers performed dances developed from those familiar from the musical suite,[31]all of which were defined by definite rhythms closely identified with each dance. These appeared as character dancesin the era of romantic nationalism.

Ballet reached widespread vogue in the romantic era, accompanied by a larger orchestra and grander musical conceptions that did not lend themselves easily to rhythmic clarity and by dance that emphasised dramatic mime. A broader concept of rhythm was needed, that which Rudolf Labanterms the "rhythm and shape" of movement that communicates character, emotion and intention,[32]while only certain scenes required the exact synchronisation of step and music essential to other dance styles, so that, to Laban, modern Europeans seemed totally unable to grasp the meaning of "primitive rhythmic movements",[33]a situation that began to change in the 20th century with such productions as Igor Stravinsky's *The Rite of Spring*with its new rhythmic language evoking primal feelings of a primitive past.[34]

Indian classical dance styles, like ballet, are often in dramatic form, so that there is a similar complementarity between narrative expression and "pure" dance. In this case, however, the two are separately defined, though not always separately performed. The rhythmic elements, which are abstract and technical, are known as *nritta*. Both this and expressive dance (*nritya*), though, are closely tied to the rhythmic system (*tala*). Teachers have adapted the spoken rhythmic mnemonic system called *bol* to the needs of dancers.

Japanese classical dance-theatre styles such as Kabukiand Noh, like Indian dance-drama, distinguish between narrative and abstract dance productions. The three main categories of kabuki are *jidaimono* (historical), *sewamono* (domestic) and *shosagoto* (dance pieces).[35]Somewhat similarly, Noh distinguishes between *Geki Noh*, based around the advancement of plot and the narration of action, and *Furyū Noh*, dance pieces involving acrobatics, stage properties, multiple characters and elaborate stage action.[36]

Participatory and social dance

Social dances, those intended for participation rather than for an audience, may include various forms of mime and narrative, but are typically set much more closely to the rhythmic pattern of music, so that terms like waltzand polkarefer as much to musical pieces as to the dance itself. The rhythm of the dancers' feet may even form an essential part of the music, as in tap dance. African dance, for example, is rooted in fixed basic steps, but may also allow a high degree of rhythmic interpretation: the feet or the trunk mark the basic pulse while cross-rhythms are picked up by shoulders, knees, or head, with the best dancers simultaneously giving plastic expression to all the elements of the polyrhythmicpattern.[37]

Cultural traditions

Africa

File:Kuduro

-

"Kuduro" (Angolan dance)   One

Ugandanyouth dance at a cultural celebration of peace

Main article: African dance   the

Dance in Africa is deeply integrated into society and major events in a community are frequently reflected in dances: dances are performed for births and funerals, weddings and wars. Web Traditional dances impart cultural morals, including religious traditions and sexual standards; give vent to repressed emotions, such as grief; motivate community members to cooperate, whether fighting wars or grinding grain; enact spiritual rituals; and contribute to social cohesiveness.[39]

Thousands of dances are performed around the continent. These may be divided into traditional, neotraditional, and classical styles: folkloricdances of a particular society, dances created more recently in imitation of traditional styles, and dances transmitted more formally in schools or private lessons.[38]:18African dance has been altered by many forces, such as European missionariesand colonialistgovernments, who often suppressed local dance traditions as licentious or distracting.[39]Dance in contemporary African cultures still serves its traditional functions in new contexts; dance may celebrate the inauguration of a hospital, build community for rural migrants in unfamiliar cities, and be incorporated into Christian church ceremonies.[39][40]

An Indian classical dancer

Asia

All Indian classical dancesare to varying degrees rooted in the *Natyashastra* and therefore share common features: for example, the *mudras* (hand positions), some body positions, leg movement and the inclusion of dramatic or expressive acting or abhinaya. Indian classical music provides accompaniment and dancers of nearly all the styles wear bells around their ankles to counterpoint and complement the percussion.

There are now many regional varieties of Indian classical dance. Dances like "Odra Magadhi", which after decades long debate, has been traced to present day Mithila, Odisharegion's dance form of Odissi(Orissi), indicate influence of dances in cultural interactions between different regions.[41]

The Punjabarea overlapping India and Pakistanis the place of origin of Bhangra. It is widely known both as a style of music and a dance. It is mostly related to ancient harvest celebrations, love, patriotism or social issues. Its music is coordinated by a musical instrument called the 'Dhol'. Bhangra is not just music but a dance, a celebration of the harvest where people beat the dhol (drum), sing Boliyaan (lyrics) and dance. It developed further with the Vaisakhi festival of the Sikhs.

The dances of Sri Lankainclude the devil dances (*yakun natima*), a carefully crafted ritual reaching far back into Sri Lanka's pre-Buddhist past that combines ancient "Ayurvedic" concepts of disease causation with psychological manipulationand combines many aspects including Sinhalese cosmology. Their influence can be seen on the classical dances of Sri Lanka.[42]

Two classical ballet dancers perform a sequence of *The Nutcracker*, one of the best known works of classical dance

*Dance at Bougival*by Pierre-Auguste Renoir(1883)

The dances of the Middle East are usually the traditional forms of circle dancing which are modernized to an extent. They would include dabke, tamzara, Assyrian folk dance, Kurdish dance, Armenian dance and Turkish dance, among others.[43][44] All these forms of dances would usually involve participants engaging each other by holding hands or arms (depending on the style of the dance). They would make rhythmic moves with their legs and shoulders as they curve around the dance floor. The head of the dance would generally hold a cane or handkerchief.[43][45]

Europe and North America

Main article: Concert dance

Folk dances vary across Europe and may date back hundreds or thousands of years, but many have features in common such as group participation led by a caller, hand-holding or arm-linking between participants, and fixed musical forms known as caroles.[46] Some, such as the maypole dance are common to many nations, while others such as the céilidh and the polka are deeply-rooted in a single culture. Some European folk dances such as the square dance were brought to the New World and subsequently became part of American culture.

Ballet developed first in Italy and then in France from lavish court spectacles that combined music, drama, poetry, song, costumes and dance. Members of the court nobility took part as performers. During the reign of Louis XIV, himself a dancer, dance became more codified. Professional dancers began to take the place of court amateurs, and ballet masters were licensed by the French government. The first ballet dance academy was the Académie Royale de Danse (Royal Dance Academy), opened in Paris in 1661. Shortly thereafter, the first institutionalized ballet troupe, associated with the Academy, was formed; this troupe began as an all-male ensemble but by 1681 opened to include women as well.[6]

20th century concert dance brought an explosion of innovation in dance style characterized by an exploration of freer technique. Early pioneers of what became known as modern dance include Loie Fuller, Isadora Duncan, Mary Wigman and Ruth St. Denis. The relationship of music to dance serves as the basis for Eurhythmics, devised by Emile Jaques-Dalcroze, which was influential to the development of Modern dance and modern ballet through artists such as Marie Rambert. Eurythmy, developed by Rudolf Steiner and Marie Steiner-von Sivers, combines formal elements reminiscent of traditional dance with the new freer style, and introduced a complex new vocabulary to dance. In the 1920s, important founders of the new style such as Martha Grahamand Doris Humphreybegan their work. Since this time, a wide variety of dance styles have been developed; see Modern dance.

African American dancedeveloped in everyday spaces, rather than in dance studios, schools or companies. Tap dance, disco, jazz dance, swing dance, hip hop dance, the lindy hopwith its relationship to rock and roll musicand rock and roll dancehave had a global influence. Dance styles fusing classical ballet technique with African-American dance have also appeared in the 21st century, including Hiplet.[47]

Latin America

Street sambadancers perform in carnival parades and contests

Dance is central to Latin Americansocial life and culture. Brazilian Samba, Argentinian tango, and Cuban salsaare internationally popular partner dances, and other national dances—merengue, cueca, plena, jarabe, joropo, marinera, cumbia, bachataand others—are important components of their respective countries' cultures.[48]Traditional Carnivalfestivals incorporate these and other dances in enormous celebrations.[49]

Dance has played an important role in forging a collective identity among the many cultural and ethnic groups of Latin America.[50]Dance served to unite the many African, European, and indigenous peoples of the region.[48]Certain dance genres, such as capoeira, and body movements, especially the characteristic *quebradas* or pelvisswings, have been variously banned and celebrated throughout Latin American history.[50]

United States

Hip hoporiginated in New York, specifically in the area known as the Bronx. It was created for those who struggled in society and didn't seem to have a voice in the community that surrounded them because of their lack of wealth. It helped those in the same situation come together and speak about difficult topics by using movement and feeling.[51]

Dance education

Dance studies are offered through the artsand humanitiesprograms of many higher education institutions. Some universities offer Bachelor of Artsand higher academic degreesin Dance. A dance study curriculum may encompass a diverse range of courses and topics, including dance practice and performance, choreography, ethnochoreology, kinesiology, dance notation, and dance therapy. Most recently, dance and movement therapy has been integrated in some schools into math lessons for students with learning disabilities, emotional/behavioral disabilities and/or attention deficit hyperactivity disorder (ADHD).[52]

A dancer practices in a dance studio, the primary setting for training in classical dance and many other styles

Occupations

Main article: List of dance occupations

Professional dancers

Professional dancers are usually employed on contract or for particular performances or productions. The professional life of a dancer is generally one of constantly changing work situations, strong competitive pressure and low pay. Consequently, professional dancers often must supplement their incomes to achieve financial stability. In the U.S. many professional dancers belong to unions (such as the American Guild of Musical Artists, Screen Actors Guild and Actors' Equity Association) that establish working conditions and minimum salaries for their members. Professional dancers must possess large amounts of athleticism. To lead a successful career, it is advantageous to be versatile in many styles of dance, have a strong technical background and to utilize other forms of physical training to remain fit and healthy.[53]

Dance teachers

Dance teachers typically focus on teaching dance performance, or coaching competitive dancers, or both. They typically have performance experience in the types of dance they teach or coach. For example, dancesport teachers and coaches are often tournament dancers or former dancesport performers. Dance teachers may be self-employed, or employed by dance schools or general education institutions with dance programs. Some work for university programs or other schools that are associated with professional classical dance (e.g., ballet) or modern dance companies. Others are employed by smaller, privately owned dance schools that offer dance training and performance coaching for various types of dance.

Choreographers

Choreographers are the ones that design the dancing movements within a dance, they are often university trained and are typically employed for particular projects or, more rarely may work on contract as the resident choreographer for a specific dance company.[54]

Competitions

An amateur dancesport competition, featuring the Viennese Waltz

A **dance competition** is an organized event in which contestants perform dances before a judge or judges for awards, and in some cases, monetary prizes. There are several major types of dance competitions, distinguished primarily by the style or styles of dances performed. Major types of dance competitions include:

- Competitive dance, in which a variety of theater dance styles, such as acro, ballet, jazz, hip-hop, lyrical, and tap, are permitted.
- Opencompetitions, that permit a wide variety of dance styles. An example of this is the TV program *So You Think You Can Dance*.
- Dancesport, which is focused exclusively on ballroomand latin dance. Examples of this are TV programs *Dancing with the Stars*and *Strictly Come Dancing*.
- Single-stylecompetitions, such as; highland dance, dance team, and Irish dance, that only permit a single dance style.

In addition, there are numerous dance competitions shows presented on televisionand other mass media.

Dance in India

Part of a serieson the

Culture of India

Ashoka

Chakra.svg

History

People

Languages[show]

Mythology and folklore[show]

Cuisine

Religion

Art[show]

Literature[show]

Music and performing arts[show]

Media[show]

Sport

Monuments[show]

Symbols[show]

- Fl India portal
  ag
  of
  India.svg
  14

- v
- t
- e

Dance in India include classical (above), semiclassical, folk and tribal.

Dance in Indiacomprises numerous styles of dances, generally classified as classical or folk.[1]As with other aspects of Indian culture, different forms of dances originated in different parts of India, developed according to the local traditions and also imbibed elements from other parts of the country.[2]

Sangeet Natya Academy, the national academy for performing arts in India, recognizes eight traditional dances as Indian classical dances,[3]while other sources and scholars recognize more.[4][5]These have roots in the Sanskrit text *Natya Shastra*,[1]and the religious performance arts of Hinduism.[6][7][8]

Folk dances are numerous in number and style and vary according to the local tradition of the respective state, ethnic or geographic regions. Contemporary dances include refined and experimental fusions of classical, folk and Western forms. Dancing traditions of India have influence not only over the dances in the whole of South Asia, but on the dancing forms of South East Asiaas well. Dances in Indian films like Bollywood Dancefor Hindi films, are often noted for freeform expression of dance and hold a significant presence in popular culture of the Indian subcontinent.[9]

Contents

Nomenclature

A classical dance is one whose theory, training, means and rationale for expressive practice is documented and traceable to ancient classical texts, particularly the *Natya Shastra*.[1][10]Classical Indian dances have historically involved a school or *guru*-*shishya parampara* (teacher-disciple tradition) and require studies of the classical texts, physical exercises and extensive training to systematically synchronize the dance repertoire with underlying play or composition, vocalists and the orchestra.[11][12]

A folk Indian dance is one which is largely an oral tradition,[13]whose traditions have been historically learnt and mostly passed down from one generation to the next through word of mouth and casual joint practice.[14]A semi-classical Indian dance is one that contains a classical imprint but has become a folk dance and lost its texts or schools. A tribal dance is a more local form of folk dance, typically found in one tribal population; typically tribal dances evolve into folk dances over a historic period.[15][16]

Origin of Dance in India

Shiva as Nataraja(Lord of Dance).

The origins of dance in India go back into the ancient times. The earliest paleolithic and neolithic cave paintings such as the UNESCO world heritage site at Bhimbetka rock sheltersin Madhya Pradesh shows dance scenes.[17]Several sculptures found at Indus Valley Civilizationarchaeological sites, now distributed between Pakistan and India, show dance figures. For example, the Dancing Girl sculptureis dated to about 2500 BCE, shows a 10.5 centimetres (4.1 in) high figurine in a dance pose.[18][19][20]

The Vedas integrate rituals with performance arts, such as a dramatic play, where not only praises to gods were recited or sung, but the dialogues were part of a dramatic representation and discussion of spiritual themes.[21][22]The Sanskrit verses in chapter 13.2 of Shatapatha Brahmana(≈800–700 BCE), for example, are written in the form of a play between two actors.[23]

The Vedic sacrifice (*yajna*) is presented as a kind of fight, with its actors, its dialogues, its portion to be set to music, its interludes, and its climaxes.

— *Louis Renou, Vedic India*[21]

The evidence of earliest dance related texts are in *Natasutras*, which are mentioned in the text of Panini, the sage who wrote the classic on Sanskrit grammar, and who is dated to about 500 BCE.[24][25]This performance arts related Sutratext is mentioned in other late Vedic texts, as are two scholars names Shilalin (IAST: Śilālin) and Krishashva (Kṛśaśva), credited to be pioneers in the studies of ancient drama, singing, dance and Sanskrit compositions for these arts.[24][26]Richmond et al. estimate the *Natasutras* to have been composed around 600 BCE, whose complete manuscript has not survived into the modern age.[25][24]

The classic text of dance and performance arts that has survived is the Hindu text *Natya Shastra*, attributed to sage Bharata. He credits the art his text systematically presents to times before him, ultimately to Brahma who created Natya-veda by taking the word from the Rigveda, melody from the Samaveda, mime from the Yajurveda, and emotion from the Atharvaveda.[27][28][29]The first complete compilation of *Natya Shastra* is dated to between 200 BCE and 200 CE,[30][31]but estimates vary between 500 BCE and 500 CE.[32]The most studied version of the Natya Shastra text consists of about 6000 verses structured into 36 chapters.[30][33]The classical dances are rooted in *Natya Shastra*.[1]

India has a number of classical Indian danceforms, each of which can be traced to different parts of the country. Classical and folk dance forms also emerged from Indian traditions, epics and mythology.[34][35]

Classical dance

Main article: Indian classical dance

Classical dance of India has developed a type of dance-drama that is a form of a total theater. The dancer acts out a story almost exclusively through gestures. Most of the classical dances of India enact stories from Hindu mythology.[36]Each form represents the culture and ethos of a particular region or a group of people.[37]

The criteria for being considered as classical is the style's adherence to the guidelines laid down in Natyashastra, which explains the Indian art of acting. The Sangeet Natak Akademicurrently confers classical status on eight Indian classical dance styles: Bharatanatyam(Tamil Nadu), Kathak(North, West and Central India), Kathakali(Kerala), Kuchipudi(Andhra), Odissi(Odisha), Manipuri(Manipur), Mohiniyattam(Kerala), and Sattriya(Assam).[38][39]All classical dances of India have roots in Hindu arts and religious practices.[6][8]

The tradition of dance has been codified in the Natyashastra and a performance is considered accomplished if it manages to evoke a rasa(emotion) among the audience by invoking a particular bhava(gesture or facial expression). Classical dance is distinguished from folk dance because it has been regulated by the rules of the Natyashastra and all classical dances are performed only in accordance with them.[40]

Bharatanatyam
Main article: Bharatanatyam
Bharatanatyam
Dating back to 1000 BC, barathanatyam is a classical dance from the South Indian state of Tamil Nadu, practiced predominantly in modern times by women. The dance is usually accompanied by classical Carnatic music.[41]Bharatnatyam is a major genre of Indian classical dancethat originated in the Hindu temples of Tamil Naduand neighboring regions.[42][43][44]Traditionally, Bharatanatyam has been a solo dance that was performed exclusively by women,[45][46]and expressed Hindu religious themes and spiritual ideas, particularly of Shaivism, but also of Vaishnavismand Shaktism.[42][47][48]

Bharatanatyam and other classical dances in India were ridiculed and suppressed during the colonial British Rajera.[49][50][51]In the post-colonial period, it has grown to become the most popular classical Indian dance style in India and abroad, and is considered to be synonymous with Indian dance by many foreigners unaware of the diversity of dances and performance arts in Indian culture.[52]

Kathakali
Main article: Kathakali
Kathakali
Kathakali (katha, "story"; kali, "performance") is a highly stylized classical dance-dramaform which originated from Keralain the 17th century.[53][54][55]This classical dance form is another "story play" genre of

art, but one distinguished by its elaborately colorful make-up, costumes and face masks wearing actor-dancers, who have traditionally been all males.[54][55]

Kathakali primarily developed as a Hindu performance art, performing plays and mythical legends related to Hinduism.[56]While its origin are more recent, its roots are in temple and folk arts such as *Kutiyattam* and religious drama traceable to at least the 1st millennium CE.[54][57]A Kathakali performance incorporates movements from the ancient martial arts and athletic traditions of south India.[54][55][56]While linked to the temple dancing traditions such as *Krishnanattam, Kutiyattam* and others, *Kathakali* is different from these because unlike the older arts where the dancer-actor also had to be the vocal artist, *Kathakali* separated these roles allowing the dancer-actor to excel in and focus on choreography while the vocal artists focused on delivering their lines.[58]

kathak dance
Kathak
Main article: Kathak

Kathak is traditionally attributed to the traveling bards of ancient northern India, known as Kathakas or storytellers.[59]The term Kathak is derived from the Vedic Sanskritword *Katha* meaning "story", and *kathaka* in Sanskrit means "he who tells a story", or "to do with stories".[59][60]Kathak evolved during the Bhakti movement, particularly by incorporating childhood and amorous stories of Hindu god Krishna, as well as independently in the courts of north Indian kingdoms.[59][61]It transitioned, adapted and integrated the tastes and Persian arts influence in the Mughal courts of the 16th and 17th century, was ridiculed and declined in the colonial British era,[51][62]then was reborn as India gained independence.[50][63]

Kathak is found in three distinct forms, named after the cities where the Kathak dance tradition evolved – Jaipur, Benaresand [[Lucky].[64]Stylistically, the Kathak dance form emphasizes rhythmic foot movements, adorned with small bells (Ghungroo), the movement harmonized to the music, the legs and torso are generally straight, and the story is told through a developed vocabulary based on the gestures of arms and upper body movement, facial expressions, stage movements, bends and turns.[50][61][65]

Kuchipudi
Main article: Kuchipudi
Kuchipudi

Kuchipudi classical dance originated in a village of Krishna districtin modern era Indian state of Andhra Pradesh.[66][67][68]It has roots in antiquity and developed as a religious art linked to traveling bards, temples and spiritual beliefs, like all major classical dances of India.[69][70][71]In its history, the Kuchipudi dancers were all males, typically Brahmins, who would play the roles of men and women in the story after dressing appropriately.[72]

Modern Kuchipudi tradition believes that Tirtha Narayana Yati and his disciple an orphan named Siddhendra Yogi founded and systematized the art in the 17th century.[73][74][75]Kuchipudi largely developed as a Hindu god Krishna-oriented Vaishnavismtradition,[76]and it is most closely related to Bhagavata Melaperformance art found in Tamil Nadu, [70]which itself has originated from Andhra Pradesh. The Kuchipudi performance includes pure dance (*nritta*),[77]and expressive part of the performance (*nritya*), where rhythmic gestures as a sign languagemime the play.[77][78]Vocalists and musicians accompany the artist, and the *tala* and *raga* set to (Carnatic music).[79]In modern productions, Kuchipudi dancers include men and women.[80]

Odissi

Main article: Odissi

Odissi

Odissi originated in the Hindu templesof Odisha– an eastern coastal state of India.[81][82]Odissi, in its history, was performed predominantly by women,[45][81]and expressed religious stories and spiritual ideas, particularly of Vaishnavism(Vishnu as Jagannath), but also of other traditions such as those related to Hindu gods Shivaand Surya, as well as Hindu goddesses (Shaktism).[83]Odissi is traditionally a dance-drama genre of performance art, where the artist(s) and musicians play out a mythical story, a spiritual message or devotional poem from the Hindu texts, using symbolic costumes,[84]body movement, *abhinaya* (expressions) and *mudras* (gestures and sign language) set out in ancient Sanskrit literature.[85]

Sattriya[edit]

Main article: Sattriya

Sattriya

Sattriya is a classical dance-drama performance art with origins in the Krishna-centered Vaishnavism monasteries of Assam, and attributed to the 15th century Bhakti movementscholar and saint named Srimanta Sankardev.[86][87][88]One-act plays of *Sattriya* are called *Ankiya Nat*, which combine the aesthetic and the religious through a ballad, dance and drama.[89][90]The plays are usually performed in the dance community halls (*namghar*[90]) of monastery temples (*sattras*).[91]The themes played relate to Krishna and Radha, sometimes other Vishnu avatarssuch as Rama and Sita.[92]

Manipuri[edit]

Main article: Manipuri dance

Manipuri

Manipuri, also known as Jagoi,[93]is named after the region of its origin – Manipur, a state in northeastern Indiabordering with Myanmar(Burma).[94][95]It is particularly known for its Hindu Vaishnavismthemes, and performances of love-inspired dance drama of Radha-Krishna called Rass Lila.[94][93][96]However, the dance is also performed to themes related to Shaivism, Shaktismand regional deities such as Umang Lai during Lai Haraoba.[97][98]The Manipuri dance is a team performance, with its own unique costumes notably the *Kumil* (a barrel shaped, elegantly decorated skirt), aesthetics, conventions and repertoire.[99]The Manipuri dance drama is, for most part, marked by a performance that is graceful, fluid, sinuous with greater emphasis on hand and upper body gestures.[100][101]

Mohiniyattam

Main article: Mohiniyattam

Mohiniyattam.

Mohiniyattam developed in the state of Kerala, gets its name from Mohini– the seductress avatarof Vishnu, who in Hindu mythology uses her charms to help the good prevail in a battle between good and evil.[102][103]Mohiniyattam follows the Lasya style described in *Natya Shastra*, that is a dance which is delicate, with soft movements and feminine.[103][104]It is traditionally a solo dance performed by women after extensive training. The repertoire of Mohiniyattam includes pure and expressive dance-drama performance, timed to sopana (slower melody) styled music,[105][106]with recitation. The songs are typically in Malayalam-Sanskrit hybrid called Manipravala.[103]

Folk and tribal dance forms

Main article: Folk dance in India

Gujarati Navaratri Garba at Ambaji Temple

Folk dances and plays in India retain significance in rural areas as the expression of the daily work and rituals of village communities.[107]

Sanskrit literature of medieval times describes several forms of group dances such as Hallisaka, Rasaka, Dand Rasakaand Charchari. The Natya Shastraincludes group dances of women as a preliminary dance performed in prelude to a drama.[108]

Bhangra, folk dance form from dancers Punjab, India.

India has numerous folk dances. Every statehas its own folk dance forms like Bihuand Bagurumbain Assam, Garba, Gagari (dance), Ghodakhund& Dandiyain Gujarat, Natiin Himachal Pradesh, Neyopa, Bacha Nagmain Jammu and Kashmir, Jhumair, Domkachin Jharkhand, Bedara Vesha, Dollu Kunithain Karnataka, Thirayattamand Theyyamin Kerala, Dalkhaiin Western Odisha, Bhangra& Giddhain Punjab, Kalbelia, Ghoomar, Rasiyain Rajasthan, Perini Dancein Telangana, Chholiyadance in Uttarakhandand likewise for each state and smaller regions in it.[109]Lavani, and Lezim, and Koli dance is most popular dance in Maharashtra.

Tribal Dances in India are inspired by the tribal folklore. Each ethnic group has its own distinct combination of myths, legends, tales, proverbs, riddles, ballads, folk songs, folk dance, and folk music.[110]

The dancers do not necessarily fall rigidly into the category of "tribal". However, these forms of dance closely depict their life, social relationships, work and religious affiliations. They represent the rich culture and customs of their native lands through intricate movements of their bodies. A wide variation can be observed in the intensity of these dances. Some involve very slight movement with a more groovy edge to it, while others involve elevated and vigorous involvement of limbs.

These dances are composed mostly on locally made instruments. Percussion instruments feature in most of these dances. Music is produced through indigenous instruments. Music too has its own diversity in these tribal dances with the aesthetics ranging from mild and soothing to strong and weighted rhythms. A few of them also have songs, either sung by themselves or by onlookers. The costumes vary from traditional saris of a particular pattern to skirts and blouses with mirror work for women and corresponding dhotis and upper-wear for men. They celebrate contemporary events, victories and are often performed as a mode of appeasing the tribal deities.

A lot of the dance styles depend upon the regional positioning of the ethnic group. Factors as small as east or west of a river result in a change of dance form even though the over-reaching look of it may seem the same. The religious affiliation affects the content of the songs and hence the actions in a dance sequence. Another major factor affecting their content are the festivals, mostly harvest.

For example, the ethnic groups from the plain land rabhas from the hilly forested areas of Assam make use of baroyat (plate-like instrument), handa (a type of sword), boushi (adze-like instrument), boumshi (bamboo flute), sum (heavy wooden instrument), dhansi. kalbansi, kalhurang, chingbakak. Traditionally, their dances are called basili. Through their dance, they express their labours, rejoicings and sorrows. Handur Basu their pseudo-war dance expresses their strength and solidarity.[111]

From a broader point of view, the different tribal dance forms, as they would be classified in the context of territory are:

Andhra Pradesh

Siddi, Tappeta Gundlu, Urumulu (thunder dance), Butta Bommalata, Goravayyalu, Garaga (Vessel Dance), Vira Ntyam (Heroic Dance), Kolatam, Chiratala Bhajana, Dappu, Puli V esham (Tiger Dance), Gobbi, Karuva, and Veedhi Bhagavatam.[112]

Thirayattam, an ethnic dance form from Kerala, India.

Arunachal Pradesh

Ponung, Sadinuktso, Khampti, Ka Fifai, Idu Mishmi (ritual) and Wancho.

Assam

Dhuliya and Bhawariya, Bihu, Deodhani, Zikirs, Apsara-Sabah.[112]

Goa

Mussoll, Dulpod or Durpod, Kunnbi-Geet, Amon, Shigmo, Fugdi, and Dhalo.

Haryana

Rasleela, Phag Dance, Phalgun, Daph Dance, Dhamaal, Loor, Guga, Jhomar, Ghomar, Khoria, Holi, Sapela.[112]

Himachal Pradesh

Chamba, Dalshone and Cholamba, Jataru Kayang, Nuala, Jhoori, Ji, Swang Tegi, Rasa.[112]

Jharkhand

Mundari dance, Santali dance.[113]

Karnataka

veeragase, Nandi Dhwaja, Beesu Kamshaley, Pata Kunitha, Bana Debara Kunitha, Pooja kunitha, Karaga, Gorawa Mela, Bhuta Nrutya, Naga Nrutya, Batte Kola, Chennu Kunitha, Maaragalu Kunitha, Kolata, Simha Nrutya,[112]Yakshagana

Kerala

Thirayattam, Padayani, Ayyappanvilakku, Vattakkali, Theyyam, Mohiniyattom, Kadhakali, Thiruvathira Kali, Ottamthullal, Kerala Folk dance, Kalamezhuthum pattum, Oppana, Marghamkali, Chavittunadakam, Mudiyettu, Dhaphumuttu, Kolkali, Pulikali, Pettathullal

Madhya Pradesh

Gaur, Muriya, Saila, Kaksar, Sugga, Banjaara (Lehangi), Matki Dance, Phul Patti Dance, Grida Dance.[112]

Manipur

Lie Haraoba Dance, Chanlam, Toonaga Lomna Dance[112]

Meghalaya

Wiking, Pombalang Nongkrem[112]

Mizoram

Cheraw, Khuallam, Chheihlam, Chailam, Tlanglam, Sarlamkai,Chawnglaizawn[112]

Maharashtra

Lavani, Koli, Tamasha, Bala Dindi & Dhangari Gaja[112]

Odisha

Naga, Ghumri,[112]Danda Nacha,[114]Chhau, Goti Pua, Dal khai, Baagha Nacha, Keisabadi

Punjab

Kikri, Sammi, Karthi, Jhumar[112]

Rajasthan

Banjaara, Ghoomar, Fire dance, Tera tali, Kachhi Ghori, Geedar[112]

Sikkim

Pang Toed Chaam (Chaam means dance) performed during the Pang Lhabsol festival in honour of the Guardian deity Khang-Chen-Dzonga, Maruni (Nepali Dance) and Tamak.[112]

Tamil Nadu

Santali Dance

Karakam, Puravai Attam, Ariyar Natanam, Podikazhi Attam, Kummi, Kavadi, Kolattam, Navasandhi, Kuravaik Koothu, Mayilaattam, Oyil Kummi, Pavakkuthu[112]

West Bengal

Santali dance, Jatra, Gazan[112]

Tribal Gypsies

Lozen, Gouyen[112]

Contemporary dance

Dance accompanied by Rabindra Sangeet, a music genre started by Rabindranath Tagore.

Contemporary dancein India encompasses a wide range of dance activities currently performed in India. It includes choreographyfor Indian cinema, modern Indian balletand experiments with existing classical and folk forms of dance by various artists.[115]

Uday Shankarand Shobana Jeyasingh have led modern Indian ballet which combined classical Indian dance and music with Western stage techniques. Their productions have included themes related to Shiva-Parvati, Lanka Dahan, Panchatantra, Ramayana among others.[116]

Dance in Bollywood Film

Main articles: Hindi dance songsand Bollywood song and dance

The presentation of Indian dance styles in film, Hindi Cinema, has exposed the range of dance in India to a global audience.[117]

Dance and song sequences have been an integral component of films across the country. With the introduction of sound to cinema in the film Alam Arain 1931, choreographed dance sequences became ubiquitous in Hindi and other Indian films.[118]

A Bollywood dance performance in Bristol.

Dance in early Hindi films was primarily modelled on classical Indian dance styles such as Kathak, or folk dancers. Modern films often blend this earlier style with Western dance styles (MTVor in Broadway musicals), though it is not unusual to see western choreography and adapted classical dance numbers side by side in the same film. Typically, the hero or heroine performs with a troupe of supporting dancers. Many song-and-dance routines in Indian films feature dramatic shifts of location and/or changes of costume between verses of a song. It is popular for a hero and heroine to dance and sing a pas de deux(a Frenchballetterm, meaning "dance of two") in beautiful natural surroundings or architecturally grand settings, referred to as a "picturisation".[119]Indian films have often used what are now called "item numbers" where a glamorous female figure performs a cameo. The choreography for such item numbers varies depending on the film's genre and situation. The film actress and dancer Helenwas famous for her cabaret numbers.[120]

Often in movies, the actors don't sing the songs themselves that they dance too, but have another artist sing in the background. For an actor to sing in the song is unlikely but not rare. The dances in Bollywood can range from slow dancing, to a more upbeat hip hop style dance. The dancing itself is a fusion of all dance forms. It could be Indian classical, Indian folk dance, belly dancing, jazz, hip hop and everything else you can imagine.[121]

Dance education

Since India's independence from colonial rule, numerous schools have opened to further education, training and socialization through dance classes,[122][123] or simply a means to exercise and fitness.[124]

Major cities in India now have numerous schools that offer lessons in dances such as *Odissi*, *Bharatanatyam*, and these cities host hundreds of shows every year.[125][126] Dances which were exclusive to one gender, now have participation by both males and females.[127] Many innovations and developments in modern practice of classical Indian dances, states Anne-Marie Geston, are of a quasi-religious type.[52]

Geographic spread

Some traditions of the Indian classical dance are practiced in the whole Indian subcontinent, including Pakistan and Bangladesh, with which India shares several other cultural traits. Indian mythologies play significant part in dance forms of countries in South East Asia, an example being the performances based on Ramayana in Javanese dances.[128]

History of dance

This article **needs additional citations for** verification. Please help improve this article by adding citations to reliable sources. Unsourced material may be challenged and removed.

Find sources: "History of dance" – news·newspapers·books·scholar·JSTOR *(May 2016) (Learn how and when to remove this template message)*

Veiled dancer, ancient Greek terracotta figurine from Myrina, ca. 150–100 BC. Louvre Museum

Ancient Greek terracotta statuette of a dancing maenad, 3rd century BC, from Taranto.

The **history of dance** is difficult to access because dance does not often leave behind clearly identifiable physical artifacts that last over millennia, such as stone tools, hunting implements or cave paintings. It is not possible to identify with exact precision when dance became part of human culture.

Contents

Early dance

The impulse to dance may have existed in early primates before they evolved into humans.[1]Dance has been an important part of ceremony, rituals, celebrationsand entertainmentsince before the birth of the earliest human civilizations. Archaeologydelivers traces of dance from prehistoric timessuch as the 30,000-year-old Bhimbetka rock shelterspaintings in Indiaand Egyptiantomb paintings depicting dancing figures from c. 3300 BC. Many contemporary danceforms can be traced back to historical, traditional, ceremonialand ethnicdances of the ancient period.

Means of social communication and bonding[edit]

Dance may have been used as a tool of social interaction that promoted cooperation essential for survival among early humans. Studies found that today's best dancers share two specific genes associated with a predisposition for being good social communicators.[2]

As folk celebrations

Main article: Folk dance

Many dances of the early periods were performed to celebrate festivals, on important or seasonal occasions such as crop harvest, or births and weddings. Such dances are found all over the world.[3]

In ceremonies and rituals

Main article: Ceremonial dance

Dance may be performed in religious or shamanic rituals, for example in rain danceperformed in times of drought. Shamans dancing for rain is mentioned in ancient Chinese texts. Dance is an important aspect of some religious rites in ancient Egypt,[4]similarly dance is also integral to many ceremonies and rites among African people.[5]Ritual dances may also be performed in temples and during religious festivals, for example the Rasa ritual dancesof India (a number of Indian classical dancesmay have their origin in ritual dances), and the Cham dancesof Tibet.[6]

As a method of healing

Another early use of dance may have been as a precursor to ecstatic trance statesin healing rituals. Dance is used for this purpose by many cultures from the Brazilian rainforestto the Kalahari Desert.[7]Medieval European *danses macabres* were thought to have protected participants from disease; however; the hysteria and duration of these dances sometimes led to death due to exhaustion.[8]

According to a Sinhalese legend, Kandyan dancesoriginated 2500 years ago, from a magic dance ritual that broke the spell on a bewitched king to cure the king of a mysterious illness.

As a method of expression

One of the earliest structured uses of dances may have been in the performance and in the telling of myths. It was also sometimes used to show feelings for one of the opposite gender. It is also linked to the origin of "love making." Before the production of written languages, dance was one of the methods of passing these stories down from generation to generation.[9]

In European culture, one of the earliest records of dancing is by Homer, whose *Iliad*describes chorea(χορεία *khoreia*). The early Greeksmade the art of dancing into a system, expressive of all the different passions. For example, the dance of the Furies, so represented, would create complete terror among those who witnessed them. The Greek philosopher, Aristotle, ranked dancing with poetry, and said that certain dancers, with rhythm applied to gesture, could express manners, passions, and actions.[citation _needed_]The most eminent Greek sculptors studied the attitudeof the dancers for their art of imitating the passion.

Asia

Shiva as Nataraja(Lord of Dance).

Indian classical dance

Main articles: Dance in Indiaand Dances of Sri Lanka

An early manuscript describing dance is the _Natya Shastra_ on which is based the modern interpretation of classical Indian dance(e.g. Bharathanatyam).

During the reign of the last Mughalsand Nawabsof Oudhdance fell down to the status of 'nautch', an unethical sensuous thing of courtesans.

Later, linking dance with immoral trafficking and prostitution, British rule prohibited public performance of dance. Many disapproved it. In 1947, India won her freedom and for dance an ambience where it could regain its past glory. Classical forms and regional distinctions were re-discovered, ethnic specialties were honored and by synthesizing them with the individual talents of the masters in the line and fresh innovations emerged dance with a new face but with classicism of the past.

In Sri Lanka, the ancient Sinhalesechronicle _Mahavamsa_ states that when King Vijayalanded in Sri Lanka in 543 BCE he heard sounds of music and dancing from a wedding ceremony. The origins of the dances of Sri Lankaare dated back to the aboriginal tribes, and to the mythological times of aboriginalyingyang twins and "yakkas" (devils). The classical dances of Sri Lanka (Kandyan dances) feature a highly developed system of tala (rhythm), provided by cymbals called thalampataa.

China

Main article: History of Chinese dance

Details from a copy of a 10th-century painting _Night Revels of Han Xizai_ by Gu Hongzhong, depicting a dancer performing a dance known in the Tang dynasty.

There is a long recorded history of Chinese dances. Some of the dances mentioned in ancient texts, such as dancing with sleeve movements are still performed today. Some of the early dances were associated with shamanic rituals. Folk dancesof the early period were also developed into court dances. The important dances of the ancient period were the ceremonial _yayue_ dated to the Zhou dynastyof the first millennium BC. The art of dance in China reached its peak during the Tang dynasty, a period when dancers from many parts of the world also performed at the imperial court.

However, Chinese operabecame popular during the Song and Yuan dynasty, and many dances were merged into Chinese opera.[10]The art of dance in women also declined from the Song dynastyonward as a result of the increasing popularity of footbinding,[11]a practice that ironically may have originated from dancing when a dancer wrapped her feet so she may dance ballet-fashion.[12][13]The best-known of the Chinese traditional dances are the dragon danceand lion dance. Lion dance was described in the Tang dynasty in form that resembles today's dance.[10]

Europe

See also: Medieval dance, Renaissance dance, and History of ballet

Pietro Longhi, *La lezione di danza* ("The Dancing Lesson"), ca 1741, Venezia, Gallerie dell'Accademia.

15th–19th centuries: from court dancing to Romanticism[edit]

The origins of ballet dancing can be traced to the Italian Renaissance courts of the 15th century. Dance masters would teach the steps to nobility and the court would participate in performances as a form of social entertainment. This practice continued for several centuries. In the 17th century, courtly balletreached its peak under the rule of King Louis XIV.[14]

By the 18th century, ballethad migrated from the French and Italian royal courts to the Paris Opéraunder the careful direction of composer/dancer Jean-Baptiste Lully. Lully sought to develop ballet into more serious art. Under his influence, the ballet was turned into a recognized art that was performed by professional dancers rather than courtiers.

During the 18th century, ballet transitioned from a courtly dance of moving images as a spectacle to performance art in its own right. Ballet performances developed around a central narrative and contained an expressive movement that revealed the relationships between characters. This dramatic style of ballet became known as the ballet d'action. The ballet d'action strove to express, for the first time, human emotions drawn directly from the dancers themselves. Masks previously worn by performers were removed so that emotional content could be derived from facial expressions.[14]

Costumes during this time were very restricting for dancers. Although a more expressive use of the body was encouraged, dancers' movements were still restricted due to heavy materials and corseted dresses. Costumes often covered a dancer's physique and made it difficult to see complex or intricate choreography. It was not until choreographer Jean Georges Noverrecalled for dance reforms in 1760 with his *Letters on Dancing and*

Ballets that costumes became more conducive. Noverre urged that costumes be crafted using lightweight fabrics that move fluidly with the body, complementing a dancer's figure. In addition, dancers wore soft slippers that fit snugly along the foot. This shoe design instilled confidence within the ballerina, daring her to dance on her toes. Naturalistic costuming allowed dancers to push the boundaries of movement, eventually rising en pointe.

The era of Romanticismproduced ballets inspired by fantasy, mystique, and the unfamiliar cultures of exotic places. Ballets that focused more on the emotions, the fantasy and the spiritual worlds, heralded the beginning of true pointe-work. Now, on her toes, the deified ballerina (embodied in this period by the legendary ballerina Marie Taglioni) seemed to magically skim the surface of the stage, an ethereal being never quite touching the ground. It was during this period that the ascending star of the ballerina quite eclipsed the presence of the poor male dancer, who was in many cases reduced to the status of a moving statue, present only in order to lift the ballerina. This sad state was really only redressed by the rise of the male ballet star Vaslav Nijinsky, with the Ballets Russes, in the early 20th century. Ballet as we know it had well and truly evolved by this time, with all the familiar conventions of costume, choreographic form, plot, pomp, and circumstance firmly fixed in place.

Early 20th century: from ballet to contemporary dance[edit]

Since the Ballets Russes began revolutionizing ballet in the early 20th century, there have been continued attempts to break the mold of classical ballet. Currently the artistic scope of ballet technique (and its accompanying music, jumper, and multimedia) is more all-encompassing than ever. The boundaries that classify a work of classical ballet are constantly being stretched, muddied and blurred until perhaps all that remains today are traces of technique idioms such as turnout.

It was during the explosion of new thinking and exploration in the early 20th century that dance artists began to appreciate the qualities of the individual, the necessities of ritual and religion, the primitive, the expressive and the emotional. In this atmosphere modern dancebegan an explosion of growth. There was suddenly a new freedom in what was considered acceptable, what was considered art, and what people wanted to create. All kinds of other things were suddenly valued as much as, or beyond, the costumes and tricks of the ballet.

Most of the early-20th-century modern choreographersand dancers saw ballet in the most negative light. Isadora Duncanthought it most ugly, nothing more than meaningless gymnastics. Martha Grahamsaw it as European and Imperialistic, having nothing to do with the modern American people. Merce Cunningham, while using some of the foundations of the ballet technique in his teaching, approached choreography and performance from a totally radical standpoint compared to the traditional balletic format.

The 20th century was indeed a period of breaking away from everything that ballet stood for. It was a time of unprecedented creative growth, for dancers and choreographers. It was also a time of shock, surprise and broadening of minds for the public, in terms of their definitions of what dance was.

The late 20th and early 21st centuries

Diagram of 20th century American dance history

After the explosion of modern dance in the early 20th century, the 1960s saw the growth of postmodernism. Postmodernism veered towards simplicity, the beauty of small things, the beauty of untrained body, and unsophisticated movement. The famous "No" manifesto rejecting all costumes, stories and outer trappings in favour of raw and unpolished movement was perhaps the extreme of this wave of thinking. Unfortunately lack of costumes, stories and outer trappings do not make a good dance show, and it was not long before sets, décor and shock value re-entered the vocabulary of modern choreographers.

By the 1980s dance had come full circle and modern dance (or, by this time, "contemporary dance") was clearly still a highly technical and political vehicle for many practitioners. Existing alongside classical ballet, the two art-forms were by now living peacefully next door to one another with little of the rivalry and antipathy of previous eras. In a cleverly designed comment on this ongoing rivalry the brilliant collaboration of Twyla Tharp (one of the 20th century's cutting edge Dance avant-gardist/contemporary) and Ballet dance was ultimately achieved. The present time sees us still in the very competitive artistic atmosphere where choreographers compete to produce the most shocking work, however, there are still glimpses of beauty to be had, and much incredible dancing in an age where dance technique has progressed further in expertise, strength and flexibility than ever before in history.

At the same time, mass cultureexperienced expansion of street dance. In 1973, famous group Jackson 5performed on television a dance called *Robot* (choreographed by postmodern[15]artist Michael Jackson) a dance form cultivated in Richmond, CA. This event and later Soul Trainperformances by black dancers (such as Don Cambell) ignited a street culture revolution, in a sense. Bboying in New York, Locking in L.A., Poping in Fresno, CA, Boogaloo in Oakland, CA, Robot in Richmond, CA, all had their own creative explosions happen around the late 60's - 70's. Each with their own histories, practices, innovators and foundations.

For the emergence of 20th-century modern dance see also: Mary Wigman, Gret Palucca, Harald Kreutzberg, Yvonne Georgi, and Isadora Duncan.

Hip-hop dancestarted when Clive Campbell, aka Kool DJ Hercand the father of hip-hop, came to New York from Jamaica in 1967. Toting the seeds of reggae from his homeland, he is credited with being the first DJ to use two turntables and identical copies of the same record to create his jams. But it was his extension of the breaks in these songs—the musical section where the percussive beats were most aggressive—that allowed him to create and name a culture of break boys and break girls who laid it down when the breaks came up. Briefly termed b-boysand b-girls, these dancers founded breakdancing, which is now a cornerstone of hip-hop dance.

Choreography (dance)

In dance, **choreography**is the act of designing dance. *Choreography* may also refer to the designitself, which is sometimes expressed by means of dance notation. A *choreographer* is one who creates dances. Dance choreographyis sometimes called *dance composition*.

Aspects of dance choreography include the compositional use of organic unity, rhythmic or non-rhythmic articulation, theme and variation, and repetition. The choreographic process may employ improvisationfor the purpose of developing innovative movement ideas. In general, choreography is used to design dances that are intended to be performed as concert dance.

The art of choreography involves the specification of human movement and form in terms of space, shape, time and energy, typically within an emotionalor non-literal context. Movement language is taken from the dance techniques of ballet, contemporary dance, jazz dance, hip hop dance, folk dance, techno, k pop, religious dance, pedestrian movement, or combinations of these.

Contents

Techniques

Dances are designed by applying one or both of these fundamental choreographic methods:

- **Improvisation**, in which a choreographer provides dancers with a *score* (i.e., generalized directives) that serves as guidelines for improvised movement and form. For example, a score might direct one dancer to withdraw from another dancer, who in turn is directed to avoid the withdrawal, or it might specify a sequence of movements that are to be executed in an improvised manner over the course of a musical phrase, as in contra dance choreography. Improvisational scores typically offer wide latitude for personal interpretation by the dancer.
- **Planned choreography**, in which a choreographer dictates motion and form in detail, leaving little or no opportunity for the dancer to exercise personal interpretation.[1]

Several underlying techniques are commonly used in choreography for two or more dancers:

- Mirroring - facing each other and doing the same
- Retrograde - performing a sequence of moves in reverse order
- Canon - people performing the same move one after the other
- Levels - people higher and lower in a dance
- Shadowing - standing one behind the other and performing the same moves
- Unison - two or more people doing a range of moves at the same time

Movements may be characterized by dynamics, such as fast, slow, hard, soft, long, and short.

www.ingramcontent.com/pod-product-compliance
Lightning Source LLC
Chambersburg PA
CBHW061521180526
45171CB00001B/278